Wine About It

ANTHOLOGY SERIES

The Prelude

edited by

Andrea Lashay & Tayler Simon

UNCUT
GEMS
AGENCY

Wine About It: The Prelude
Edited by Andrea Lashay and Tayler Simon

First edition
ISBN: 979-8-9986741-0-5

Concept developed by Andrea Lashay
Brand design by Maya Wang
Cover design by Tayler Simon
Interior design by Tayler Simon

Published by Liberation is Lit, LLC
liberationislit.com

You deserve the space to wine about it

Contents

Introduction

Prelude Edition

Pair with 2018 Ericka O Syrah

I am not alone.

That's something I had to keep reminding myself of over the years—especially while navigating heartbreak, healing, and all the mess in between.

The journey of self-love, identity, reflection, and self-trust is filled with learning and unlearning. But let's be real: when you're in it, people don't always applaud your resilience. Sometimes they call it complaining. And when that happens, you start asking yourself: *Is this really a safe space if I'm judged for being honest? If people treat my survival like a burden? If their peace depends on me being quiet?*

For a long time, I was lost in my own freedom. I grew up in a strict, unsupportive environment, and when I finally got out, I had no blueprint for how to be free. There was still trauma—but somehow, I found pockets of safety in it.

I've survived sexual assault, college chaos, rocky relationships, exploring my sexuality, and even sabotaging myself a few too many times. Through all of that, I discovered that I *could* still be free, I could still be safe—maybe not with other people, but within myself.

Still, being that girl who's "always going through something" made me a target for pity and judgment. People made me feel like I was doing too much when I couldn't afford brunch or skipped events because I had bills and debt and food to pay for. They saw my honesty as whining. But I wasn't whining—I was trying to understand the weight of freedom. If freedom sounds too cliché, imagine the responsibility that comes with that freedom. Yeah, that's what I was navigating while others were competing with me. I was being responsible for my honesty, for my choices, for my ability to choose.

Not having close relationships with my parents or extended family, paired with social anxiety and only a handful of friends, meant I had no one to blame. It was all on me. If I wanted to keep going, I had to believe in myself. I had to choose me. And some days, that meant leaning on therapy. Other days, I shut down, played nice, or drowned in vices. I filled journals and repeated the same patterns until even my own words got tired.

At one point, I thought writing a book would make people understand me. But then I realized—most people don't need a book; they just need space. Safe space. A space to speak, share, release. They don't always want sympathy—they want to *feel seen.*

Not everyone wants to be a writer. But we all have stories. And sometimes, the people who "whine" the most are also the ones who still see the good in others. That was me. Always trying to help, fix, and understand. But I needed to break those habits that kept me stuck in cycles.

So I did something different. I created a space where people can creatively share their stories and the wisdom they gained—without having to be perfect, polished, or published authors.

This is how *Wine About It* was born.

Instead of pouring my heart out online for free, I decided to build a sanctuary for stories—especially for those who've never called themselves writers but have something powerful to say. A place for those who've endured, grown, and are still figuring it out.

As a Black woman, that's the only lens I know, so for this *Prelude*, I opened submissions exclusively to other Black women. We received stories from women of all ages, and that's when Tayler and I realized this felt like a collective coming-of-age moment.

I didn't grow up in church. I didn't play sports. I carry a lot of family and social trauma. But even in all that, I've learned to create. And through that creation, I found community.

I read a quote once that said, "You're either a victim or a creator." That's when it clicked. I refused to let my pain define me. I chose to create.

This anthology is for those who chose creativity over a victim mindset. It's for the ones navigating pain, love, doubt, trauma, identity—and still choosing to show up. It's for anyone who's ever felt misunderstood but decided to keep writing their story anyway.

Pour yourself a glass of wine and flip through these pages. Let these stories help you see yourself, question what you've been taught, and reconnect with the parts of you that are still healing.

This is not just a book.

This is a safe space.

And you're welcome here.

Cheers to resilience,

Andrea

Forewarned is to be Forearmed

by Glenis Redmond
Pair with 2020 Theopolis Vineyard Petite Sirah

Beware of the shut-eye that does not sleep. Beware of
ground glass in grits. Beware of the evil eye and the
evil finger. Beware of standing beside yourself.
Beware of being an antennae picking up everyone's
feelings, leaving yours undeciphered.
Beware of tainted land—weighted with deliberate
blood spill. Beware those who work the root. Beware
of Iron Pyrite friends—don't be taken in by Fool's
Gold. It only glitters but has not worth. Beware the
fault-finders, bamboozlers, and losers.
Beware of feeling sorry for sorry. Beware of those
who ghost you. They were never there in the first
place. Beware of America's amnesia—false promises,
buildings erected without reconciling the African
Holocaust.
Beware cries for unity that ignore division's roots.
Beware the "you need to get over it." Beware of bad
checks deposited on your behalf.
Beware of seeing others' high selves when they only
present their lowest. Beware the naked man handing
you a coat. He wants what you can't afford to
give—your soul.
Beware of doctors who don't listen. They practice on
you without listening to you. They will kill you and
ask—how did that happen?
Beware of putting others before yourself. Beware of
dulling your intuition. Beware of giving arrogant
ignorance a pass.

Beware pushing override too often—one day, you won't rise.

Only Happy Birthdays

by Yaz Balogun
Pair with B. Stuyvesant Heritage

I cried on my 1st birthday
Or at least I think I did
All babies cry so it's a safe bet
I probably cried because the music was loud
Hell, I could've cried because the sky was blue

I cried on my 7th birthday
Happy tears because I got the Bratz cake I wanted
Then sad tears when they cut the cake
I think that was the first time I really understood
That I can't have my cake and eat it too

I cried on my 13th birthday
Technically it was the night before
The perm sat on my head a few minutes too long
So I spent the night picking scabs out of my scalp
And begging my mom to please let me go natural

I cried on my 16th birthday
My dress didn't fit right
My wig didn't look right
My life didn't feel right
Being alive didn't feel right

I cried on my 17th birthday
Happy and sad and anxious tears
I was going to college for free
I was going to college to be free

I was going to college to find me

I cried on my 18th birthday
I was a whole adult in the real world
I even had friends and family who loved me
I know they should've been happy tears
But they tasted bitter more than sweet

I cried on my 21st birthday
I still couldn't believe I was in my twenties
I had never let myself look past my teens
Never let myself imagine being in pain for that long
Didn't know how to imagine life without that pain

I cried on my 22nd birthday
But this time they were only happy tears
I cried because I loved myself, I loved my life
I cried because I believed in my bright future
I cried for the girl who was afraid to see this future

I'm probably gonna cry on my 23rd birthday
I hope they'll be happy tears again
I hope I cry more happy tears before then
I hope I feel a lot of other emotions too
But, most of all, I hope to have only happy birthdays

Raise a Glass

by Yaz Balogun
Pair with 2018 Bordini Barbaresco DOCG

I'm not a stranger to pain
I'm painfully aware of how inevitable she is
I wish I could say she was just an acquaintance
Not a permanent resident in my body and mind
Paying rent in tears and sleepless nights
I can tell you all the bad she's done
But I don't like to talk shit about my friends
What else would you call someone
Who has seen you at your worst and stuck around
Watched you ugly cry on New Year's Eve
Then fall asleep by the toilet after 12 too many
Heard you say the last I love you
Before it turned into I will never forgive you
Held your hand through the stages of grief
As you begged and pleaded to take their place
Given you something to feel besides numb
When everything meant nothing for months
Kept you company in the darkest of tunnels
As you dragged yourself slowly toward the light
I understand if you don't like pain
But she's my day one, my biggest motivator
The least I can do is call her a friend
After everything she's done for me, for all of us
So let's raise a glass to our homegirl, pain
Thank you, fuck you, and I'll see you again soon.

Diary of a Hopeless Romantic

by Yaz Balogun

I believe in true love. The kind of love that makes you smile uncontrollably when you hear a song. The kind of love that you feel in your belly and in your bones. The kind of love that justifies your past mistakes because they led you to this. The kind of love that gives you the courage to look in the mirror a bit longer. The kind of love that makes you wonder how you lived without it. The kind of love that you want to share with your kids and pray that they feel it someday. The kind of love that feels crafted by a divine consciousness because it's almost surreal.

But I also believe in heartache. The kind of pain that turns your whole world upside down. The kind of pain that makes you weep all night until your lips are cracked and the bags under your eyes are carrying your sorrow. The kind of pain that makes you want to drown in your tears just to feel something. The kind of pain that makes you so sick to your stomach that you lose your appetite. The kind of pain that makes you wish your heart would just stop beating altogether. The kind of pain that makes you wonder how anyone survived long enough to write about it.

I'm No Superhuman

by Mikeya Janee'

Pair with 2021 "Solis" Malbec, Cahors AOC, France

The Intro

As women, there are many ways we neglect our needs and desires. Most of us identify ourselves as multipliers without being mindful of what we are receiving or the lack thereof. Typically, it takes something drastic to happen, like a bad breakup, for us to say, "I'm going to put myself first." Well... this is my "bad breakup but dang I really need to heal" story. These next few pages are excerpts from my digital music diary: The Heart Chamber. It consists of creative materials, memories, and declarations that led me to produce the music that my community base has grown to love. Maybe because it's so raw, authentic, and straight to the point. Definitely not giving demure, but more so, "I've had enough and it's time to make a change." It's very much giving "I bleed too." And it is my hope that, after reading this short story, you will not only join this community, but you will embrace the fact that, in this season, you must surrender the lifestyle of being a superhuman and put yourself first. Enjoy!

The Climax

It was my unhealthy attachment issues versus his sense of ego and entitlement. The fuel of this war was fear: fear of what life would look like without our understanding, yet toxic, nine-year bond. Before he came into my life, I hadn't dealt with anyone who made me feel safe to be myself. I would even say that I was the first girl who made him feel he could do anything he put his mind to. I've always been a determined individual, but for some reason, letting go emotionally of a taken man was a challenge. To be fair, I never met up with him once while he had a girlfriend. Even the guys I dealt with in the past didn't have physical access to me, but I would always leave the door open to let them peek their heads in and give me false hope for the future. They would even leave the door cracked for me sometimes too—until the summer of 2021.

He had just sent me a text after ignoring me for two days straight. You see, although I was an emotional side chick, I had never been afraid to ask the hard questions, hence why he ghosted me. I asked him if he was still with his girlfriend. No response! What was the text he sent? Well, according to him, "our song" came up on his music playlist while working out at the gym, and he decided to send it to me. But that sent me THROUGH THE ROOF. I texted, "You're confused," and that sent HIM through the roof. Now it's time to argue! Y'all know about those arguments that have you walking three miles up the street, and you didn't even realize you walked three miles up the street? Well, it was one of those. My thesis and question to him was, "What do you want?" His response made me feel delusional for even asking him that question, as if he didn't randomly send me the song that bonded us together while having a full-blown girlfriend. It was the first time I had experienced his narcissistic behavior. As a result, I hung up the phone mid-scream, went into my house, grabbed the keys, and drove thirty minutes to the closest Verizon store to change my number.

The Audacity

I'd be lying if I said that, after that argument, I no longer wished we could be together someday. I still held onto that hope. But simultaneously I began resting in the fact that love is about respect, and it was time to let go. I hoped the sentiments were the same on the other side, but to my surprise they weren't. Unfortunately, the audacity had increased since we last spoke and so did his ego and entitlement. See message exchange below from the day I knew he had me fucked up:

May 17, 2022 at 7:42 pm (via Instagram DM)

Him: "ARe YoU StiLL A VirGIn???

Me: I'll answer your question if you answer mine—are you still with your girlfriend?

Him: Yes I am

Me: *sent shocked GIF* but proceeded to tell him that I was still a virgin.

Him: okay

and then it hit me.......

The Moment

May 18, 2022 at 6:33 am (via Instagram DM)

"I really want to take a moment to share my heart with you. I love you deeply (you know that already). I love you so much that I disciplined myself to not text you on your birthday so I wouldn't be a distraction or be in the way of your relationship. The goal is to be 'friends' but that's not something realistic for us right now.... well, not for me anyway. Maybe later in life. When you asked me if I was a virgin, it hurt my feelings, because to me it seems like that's a big deal for you. And I wonder would you love me less if I did lose it to someone else? That's not your first time asking me that. And I'm not 100% sure why you asked me, but I think it's so unfair that you're thinking about me having sex with someone when you literally have a girlfriend. You're literally giving your time, love, sex, and devotion to someone. You're literally committed to someone and it isn't me. It was never me! Commitment was something you never gave me. Something that I'm still trying to cope with while supporting your decision... that's love. This shit isn't easy, but I'm learning to forgive you every chance I get. And not just you, but every guy that decided to be with someone other than me, but is still so concerned about me being a virgin. This is something eventually ima have to go to therapy for because the shit runs deep. I suffer from deep rejection issues. And though I have tough skin, I'm no superhuman. I bleed just like you. So if you love me and I know you do, please consider where I am in life before you ask me a question like that."

His response was actually more mature than I thought it would be. He was very encouraging and supportive of what I said. Before this moment, I was so afraid to stand up for myself, because I was afraid of what he or any guy would say if I spoke up. But something triggered my soul when he replied, "Okay." It's like he just wanted to make sure I wasn't doing anything while he did whatever he wanted. God truly empowered me in this moment. He gave me exact instructions on when to send it: eeeaarrlllyyy in the morning. He just so happened to be in the DM while I was sending it, reviewing his message because guilt had sunk in, I assume. As soon as I sent the message, "seen" popped up on the screen, and there was nowhere to run or hide. I left the DM that day feeling proud that I had stood up for myself. More importantly, I felt empowered leaving the DM, knowing that no one owns me! This was the moment I began setting myself free from anyone's idea of who they wanted me to be or any egotistical ideas they had about me sharing my body.

The Self-Care Bullet Points

- Accept people for who they are, then make a decision.

- Set boundaries with yourself to yield much progress.

- Accept and receive who you're positively evolving into.

- Don't judge yourself while you're unlearning certain behaviors.

- Respect people's journeys but never neglect your own.

- Journal your prayers. It's documentation of your spiritual journey.

- There's much power in knowing when to be still and silent.

- Learn from the past, live in the present, leverage for your future.

- Embrace awkward moments. It helps you to discover your niche.

- Access is responsibility. Are the ones you've given access responsible?

Falling in Love: The Gift that Keeps on Keeping On

by Curtrell Gadson
Pair with Aslina Chenin Blanc

Answering the call of healing allowed me to do some beautiful things last year. It allowed me to fall in love dozens of times. The endearing arms that caught me so graciously were my own, and the very practices and rituals that were once lost became found again.

I went through a period of remembrance last year that revived my love for writing. At my first healing justice retreat, we were tasked with writing a poem. The poem was titled "I Am From…" and was accompanied by prompts that urged us to explore where we were from through our senses and ancestral roots. There was something so raw and intimate about the act of drafting a poem, sharing it with everyone, being celebrated aloud, and hearing folks share snippets that resonated with them most. Truly a liberating experience.

Later that evening, while laying in bed reflecting on the day and the resonant exercise of authoring the poem, I had the most magical experience. A core memory from my childhood was unlocked, and I reverted back to a nine-year-old version of myself writing a poem in her diary. Awestruck by the out-of-body quest, I began to tear up and was suddenly overcome with emotion. Before that moment, the memory was so distant that I had not known that any of this actually took place. It wasn't until I saw that little moon pie face with long, thick black ponytails laying in her bed writing in her purple fuzzy covered diary that I got from the book fair, that I knew that this was actually part of a past reality. The unlocked memory was welcomed with the smell of my childhood home—a mixture of stale cigarette smoke and Pine Sol and an unexpected energy transfer from my younger self of invisibility and loneliness that began to fade as soon as I saw her.

Life had "life'd" so much that I had become disconnected from who I was and was divinely created to be. Answering that call of healing took me on a journey down memory lane and helped me to reconnect, rediscover, and remember. Seeing that younger version of myself grew me in ways I hadn't yet experienced. I developed an immense amount of empathy and compassion internally, and it felt so damn good. Like the warmest hug, I was being seen and held by the person who mattered most—myself. And that was so healing. From that moment on, I have made a conscious effort to experience more warm embraces with the younger versions of myself, leaving me falling even deeper.

After making that declaration to myself, I began to see myself in all sorts of ways while partaking in the most mundane tasks. I remember once having yet another out-of-body bird's eye view experience with myself in the middle of a brainstorming session. I stared at myself in pure admiration with subtle amusement thinking, "Wow, who is this person?!" I had the distinct pleasure of seeing my manifestation of myself growing in an audacious and confident way play out in real time right before my eyes. What a gift. And sometimes, with such a special gift, you fall even further in love.

The admiration came into play because my whole life I had hidden behind the shell that kept me meek and small. Shying away from others but also self. It would steal my confidence and my youth. It was heavy and made me miss out on who I'd always been. And who I was created to be started to break through, and I began to feel light and free. With that liberating energy, I fell even deeper.

The bird's eye view was yet another warm endearing hug to that young and tender version of myself. While I was in total amazement and shock of who I was staring back at... there was a part of me that felt sadness that I soon came to realize stemmed from grief. A mourning of the only version of me I've ever known. She had served me so well through life up until that very point. I could sense the departure and what felt like a goodbye was simple, well done.

At the beginning of last year I ran across a lot of chatter online about how women were all suffering from a self-induced drought and going long periods of time without physical intimacy because men were falling short of meeting their emotional needs. Unbeknownst to me, I was not the only one suffering this fate. This had become a norm for me over the years, as I would oftentimes do long stints of abstinence for the very same reason. In my twenties, I began to de-center men in the pursuit of romantic relationships and shifted gears to centering myself and all the various areas of my life that gave me the most pleasure. I found myself fully leaning into this new approach to thriving in life through the romanticization of all the things. From the most mundane everyday task that turned into a routine of pausing and pouring into me, to the bliss that beamed as I engaged with myself, my tribe, and community in the most intimate and joyful ways. I had embarked on a journey that allowed me to lean into the erotic of life, stretching me in ways I didn't know I could expand.

After many years of centering myself and other facets of my life, I began to confront my very real need for physical intimacy, connection, and companionship. The realization that I had always neglected those needs—and was even unaware of my desires—was so jarring to me. It dawned on me that decentering romantic relationships came at its own cost if you didn't engage in casual flings.

Audre Lorde taught us that the exploration and consideration of the erotic is a source of power and information that women have access to tap into but are socialized not to utilize. In her essay, "The Uses of the Erotic: The Erotic as Power," Lorde describes how the erotic has often been reduced to pornography in western societies. She states:

> *But the erotic offers a well of replenishing and provocative force to the woman who does not*

fear its revelation, nor succumb to the belief that sensation is enough.

The erotic has often been misnamed by men and used against women. It has been made into the confused, the trivial, the psychotic, the plasticized sensation. For this reason, we have often turned away from the exploration and consideration of the erotic as a source of power and information, confusing it with its opposite, the pornographic. But pornography is a direct denial of the power of the erotic, for it represents the suppression of true feeling. Pornography emphasizes sensation without feeling. The erotic is a measure between the beginnings of our sense of self and the chaos of our strongest feelings.

This resonated with me as I had embarked on my own journey of self-exploration and healing by engaging in radical pleasure. I decided that I had needs and desires that were imperative for my evolution and began to take agency over my immediate needs for physical and emotional intimacy. Using the erotic as power, I set out to care for my whole self in a safe and consensual way with one I trusted. As liberating as this all felt to initiate, this was still very much uncharted territory for someone who didn't prioritize her needs often. In doing so, here's what this source of power and information taught me about myself:

I'm a feeler and that's okay… I found myself navigating all the familiar big feelings that would arise when in an emotionally and physically intimate relationship with another person, but the context here was different, and I wanted to be intentional with how I showed up for myself and my lover. This newly-tapped power allowed me to embrace and lean into being my most authentic self and letting the emotions and feelings come and go as they pleased. In the past, I'd show up avoidant and ridicule myself for even feeling. The suppression of the erotic served as a blockage for me exploring and fully embodying who I was created to be—an empath. My therapist told me once in a Reiki session that my life's mission and purpose is to be able to feel things and then correct the system that causes the feeling. Years later, I actually heard her and that statement for the first time.

Each big O, self-induced or otherwise, came with a gold mine of knowledge and clarity. Knowledge and clarity of my capacity to show up as the empath I was born to be in every facet of my life. I'm a feeler and, when I lean in, I'm a powerful force to be reckoned with. It's when I feel more free and aligned with who I was always meant to be.

When women fully embody their feminine energy and fully engage in the erotic acts of all kinds, sexual or otherwise, they capture the essence of liberation and healing. We should tap into the power that lies within when we dive heart first into the many pleasures that lie before us. The power of self-discovery while engaging in these acts, the power of taking up space, and the power of prioritizing and satisfying the many desires of our hearts serves us. It teaches us valuable lessons in how to nurture and care for self and community. It gives the gift of discernment when navigating life.

While my healing journey in the last year has been the most challenging, it has also been the most awakening. Having the pleasure and privilege of an outpouring of support from my tribe, community, and dearest family and friends, delivered the sweetest pleasure of them all—to fall in love with myself and all that life has to offer me over and over again. What a gift.

Beneath the Sentiments

by Annait LJ
Pair with 2021 Bayani Reserve - Pinot Noir (Stoney Wines)

Author Note:
Sentiment: a view of—or attitude toward—a situation or
event; an opinion.
"The child knows the sentiments of a lackluster parent."

Sometimes I wonder how different the world really was when my parents were born. What was the life they envisioned before I came along? Did my mother plan to be financially dependent on her children? Did my father intend to live without any means of survival until his mid 40s? How had my conception uprooted the future they never got to achieve?

And why did they make it my problem?

Like everyone else in the world, I had no choice in being here on this lovely planet. Until I got my first taxable job at 15, the modicum of control in my grasp was minimal. I could pay for a phone that routinely got checked to make sure I wasn't being "fast." Truth be told, I wasn't interested in boys or anything they had to offer. Talking to my friends and reading books and learning things about women that my mother wouldn't teach me was all I cared about.

In her eyes, though, I had the potential to be fast, and that's just as bad.

Now I know that was just a projection of her reality when she was my age. After all, she had me when she just turned 19, and I'm her second child.

I could also put gas in my mom's car because she didn't have any money to spare. Somehow, the moment income came into my hands, she expected it to be outstretched toward her own. My money was her money. Her worries were mine. Her financial immaturity became mine to scold.

Occasionally, I would have a chance to buy something I actually wanted, only to find out my mother spent the money in our "joint" account—an account funded by me, myself, and I.

This was the first time I realized my mother was human, capable of doing wrong.

Money is a fickle thing and is quick to change relationships, for better or for worse. It's best to avoid any dealings with financial exchanges, especially among family.

What could I say, though? No?

I tried to conceptualize what the outcome would be if I did voice that dangerous thought. Most days, I rode the bus to work, so she couldn't hold transportation over my head. I paid her phone bill and my own, so she couldn't take that away. Grounding me wasn't a solution, because I liked being at home and reading. She wouldn't put me out of the house.

So what could she use? Guilt. Fear. Pressure.

It was *my* money, but she used it to pay *our* bills, to keep a roof over me *and* my brothers' heads. I wouldn't want them to lack food or electricity or a home, right? Never mind the fact that I was changing most of their diapers and feeding them and helping with their homework and fighting off their bullies. I'd already crossed the line from sisterhood into co-parenting, so their wellbeing was a prime concern of mine (and still is, if I'm being honest).

Not to mention, I had intimate knowledge of being without those luxuries. Nine-year-old me, going to the red shelter on the south side of Martin Luther King Boulevard in Atlanta, Georgia, knew what it was like to have nothing except the grace of others.

I could be that grace. For my brothers. For my family.

Who cares about what I want? It's just a paycheck.

I now know it was never just that.

It was a contract of self-betrayal that asked for more, not caring if there was enough to keep me on my feet.

It was always "I'll pay you back" and never "I lack financial literacy and need a lesson in accountability." It was always one thing or another, and yet, it was never just her.

This life lesson opened my eyes and gave me a chance to step back and observe, and truthfully, I've been observing ever since. People. The things they say. The actions they take. All the things they try to use to fill in the gaps between reality and delusion. I don't recall being a talkative child overall, but I remember the moment I went silent.

It was eerie, being my own company, and thriving within the walls built in my mind. My mother would say things, I'd register them, and then I would store them away. I thought that was the healthiest outcome, and I kept that up for 10 years. Even as I stepped out of my mother's home at 18, joined the military, went to college, got married, got divorced, deployed overseas, and came back, I was silent.

Any battle I endured was birthed in a void of indifference and died in a sea of acceptance. I've gone through a lot, and there was a lot of anger to process, but I was never angry at the circumstances. Most of the time, it felt like an out-of-body experience where I was barely there to participate.

I was idle.

Unenthused.

Placated.

But I learned. I learned a lot from the parent who was present and the one who tried a little too late. Understanding finances became my safe space. Holding space for others to truly understand them became my addiction. Understanding myself became my salvation.

I can see all the components that shape me, good and bad, and I've come to terms with the fact that I'm only human. I study hard in school. K-dramas reign supreme as entertainment. Going on runs raises my endorphins. Writing books fills me with a sense of accomplishment. I love myself in every form. Making friends, stepping outside of the walls I built up, and breathing fresh air make me feel alive.

And all I want to do is live.

For myself.

Selfishly. Without the sentiments of a childhood not meant for a child to endure.

I can acknowledge that things can and always will be worse than the things I've gone through. They can also be better. But no matter the circumstance, it all makes us human.

I'm thankful I'm here and that I can live. I don't expect life to be easy or a breeze, but it will unequivocally be mine.

I intend to make sure of it.

The Miraculous Journey of a Princess: From Cellular Beginnings to Divine Purpose

by Tracey Oakman
Pair with 2023 Corazón Moon Mountain Gewürztraminer

In the intricate tapestry of life, every thread has a purpose, every stitch a story. Were you aware that all human life, at its most primal stage, begins as a princess? Yes, you read that correctly. In the microscopic realm of cellular genesis, we all start our journey as female, until that miraculous moment when the Y chromosome makes its grand entrance. This biological ballet sets the stage for the incredible story I'm about to share with you—my story. This happens to be a tale that begins with the "why" and concludes with the "X," with God serving as the eternal X factor throughout this remarkable odyssey.

As we embark on this narrative journey, let's pause to reflect on the wisdom found in Proverbs 3:5-6: "Trust in the Lord with all your heart, and do not lean on your own understanding. In all your ways acknowledge him, and he will make straight your paths." These words have been my guiding light, illuminating the darkest corners of my life and leading me to where I stand today.

I am Tracey Oakman, and as a former young princess myself, I've always known that my calling in life was to touch the lives of other young princesses facing similar challenges. The reason I can assist so many with varying lifestyles is that I've experienced the dizzying highs and the crushing lows that adulthood so fervently thrusts upon us. My journey has equipped me with a unique perspective and an unwavering empathy that allows me to connect with those I serve on a profound level.

Let me take you back to where it all began—Lefrak City, Queens. Picture a van with a mysterious scorpion emblem roaming the streets. At its helm was none other than Deaconess Oakman, my mother, a modern-day Pied Piper leading children not to peril, but to praise. "Let the little children come to me," Jesus said (Matthew 19:14), and Deaconess Oakman took these words to heart, scooping up neighborhood kids faster than you could say "Amen." For those young souls, it was a choice between running like Usain Bolt or receiving a bolt of spiritual lightning. Many of these children, without my mother's intervention, might have paved their way to foster homes, detention centers, or worse. Instead, they found salvation, proving that sometimes a scorpion can indeed lead you to the Savior. My mother saved countless lives with her love and compassion, embodying the very essence of Matthew 19:14.

New York City was like a jungle sometimes, but thanks to Deaconess Oakman, we were able to hear The Message. Her influence on my life and the lives of others cannot be overstated. If you were to ask me for validation of my theory about the impact one person can have, I would simply let my mother spread a little love in your direction. As for me, I am now the proud owner of Princess Empowerment, established in 2021, and Boys to Men, added in 2023. I'm blessed with three beautiful children—twins Shane and Shyianne, and my youngest, Mezziah. I'm also a grandmother to seven wonderful grandchildren—Knox, Swayze, Hendrick, Adonis, Marlee, Goddess, and Empress. This is my story, a testament to the power of faith, perseverance, and divine intervention.

My journey in childcare began even before I reached adulthood. I was a good kid, blessed with a great life. For 11 years, I ran a home daycare, and the proceeds helped me raise my beautiful children. I named it Odessa's Love School, a living tribute to my mother, who was my first encounter with a great leader and a woman of God. You've probably heard the saying, "It takes a village to raise a child." Well, my mother was the chief of that village, and I've grown to become what many call the child whisperer.

Throughout my career, I've worked in numerous daycare systems but often found myself at odds with their quality of care and overall approach. These experiences didn't resonate with my spirit or meet my standards for childcare. After several such encounters, I realized I had to take matters into my own hands.

Life, however, isn't always a fairy tale, even for princesses. I faced my share of dragons along the way. I fell off course in my college pursuits, despite my determination. My focus wavered as I got caught up in the distractions of my social circle. Then came a relationship with a man who I thought loved me but instead made me feel horrible about myself. His emotional abuse plunged me into a spiraling depression, leaving me in a dark place I never thought I'd escape. But as Proverbs 3:5-6 reminds us, we must trust in the Lord with all our hearts and not lean on our own understanding. And true to His word, God made my paths straight, leading me to Queen Akua Omitola Divine and her Avatar Essentials store—a divine appointment that would change everything. Queen Akua Omitola Divine ran an organization called "The Return of the Goddess Sister Circles," which became the inspiration for my program, Princess Empowerment.

Princess Empowerment was born at St. John Baptist Church with a mission to prevent young girls from being mean and abusive to each other. Today, we facilitate the program out of One Columbia, where Xavier Blake serves as the executive director. I'm forever grateful to Darion McCloud for making this amazing connection possible. As for the boys who wanted to participate but couldn't because it was for the princesses (and the young queens were not having that intrusion), we started Boys to Men. Jamal Washington answered the call to develop these young boys into men, and I'm equally grateful for his dedication.

Our programs are diverse and impactful. We incorporate breathing techniques and affirmations to help our young participants center themselves and build self-confidence. One of our most powerful initiatives is the ILAC program, which stands for "I am Lovable and Capable." In this exercise, girls color paper plates and make them beautiful. They then discuss their problems and symbolically rip the plates.

In smaller groups, they talk through these issues and work on solutions. Finally, they repair the plates, making them whole again. They create, they destroy, and then—like phoenixes rising from the ashes—they rebuild. This powerful metaphor teaches our young ladies that, even though they face problems, they remain lovable and capable. Just like the tattered but repaired plate, they are still beautiful and worthy. This isn't just arts and crafts; it's an introduction to life skills, teaching resilience and self-worth in the face of adversity.

We also run mindfulness programs focusing on gratitude and mindful eating. Our summer camps offer a variety of activities, including recycling projects, animation studios, and music programs. Community service is a cornerstone of our work. We've fed the homeless, served nursing homes and the Ronald McDonald House, and even gone Christmas caroling in neighborhoods.

As I stated earlier, my journey hasn't been without its dark moments. There were times when I abused drugs, suffered abuse from my significant other, and although I never wanted to end my life, the weight of depression often made me want to leave this world. But God delivered me from this spirit of depression. I had a praying mother, and as the Bible says, the prayers of the righteous availeth much. I owe my recovery and success to the children I serve, my family, and most importantly, to God. As Jeremiah 29:11 proclaims, "'For I know the plans I have for you,' declares the Lord, 'plans to prosper you and not to harm you, plans to give you hope and a future.'" My story is living proof of this promise, a testament to the power of faith, family, and the unyielding spirit of a true princess warrior. I now work at a wonderful school, The Amazing Learning Academy, under the direction of Barbara Scott. She saw my gift and paved the way for my vision. Thank you for sharing your tiara, Barbara.

To all the princesses out there, young, and old, remember this: Your worth is not determined by your circumstances, but by the love of a God who knew you before you were formed in the womb. You are lovable, you are capable, and you have the power to change lives—starting with your own. Embrace your royal heritage, wear your visible crown with pride, and go forth and make your unique mark on the world. For, in God's kingdom, every princess has the potential to become a queen, leading others with love, compassion, and unwavering faith.

Hellcats

by Dr. Ebony Toussaint
Pair with 2022 White Blend Daisy (FLYgirl Wines)

She sat humming a familiar tune about how good
God had been to her. Her warm brown skin held on
to the many laughs over the years at the seams where
her cheeks met her brown eyes. Her hands were
covered in white all-purpose baking flour from
making the best biscuits that I had to have every time
I came home from college. She was my first stop, and
I could always smell the biscuits baking in the oven
from her front porch. Her biscuits were so good that
our family would later have a Biscuit Bake Off of
sorts, trying to determine whose recipe tasted the
same as hers. No biscuit came close.

I didn't realize it at the time of her death, but I
didn't know much about my grandmother. I did know
that she loved me. I was her pride and joy. Her room
was covered in the evidence of her love for me at the
time of her transition. She had kept items I had long
forgotten. A piece of art I made in Sunday School, a
spelling bee award, and a calendar with my photo.
How could my grandmother leave with so much left
to teach me about life and love? It felt like we had
unfinished business. I don't know how well the
Kübler-Ross framework aligns with my Gullah
Geechee cultural heritage or my heritage within the
African diaspora. There must be another word to

describe our love. Any word I can think of falls short of truly capturing our connection.

A short time before her death, my grandmother and I sat with my father. He told stories of growing up in the back of the Juke Joint that my grandmother owned and operated. He said she carried a razor blade and smoked cigarettes. I sat staring at my grandmother with my mouth wide open, while she let out one of the most guttural laughs I'd ever heard. Struggling to get a single word out, I simply asked, "Grandma Tiny?" to which she responded, "I was a hellcat." I still wouldn't have believed it if I hadn't seen photographic evidence of my grandma looking like the cover of a Tupac album.

My grandmother died shortly after this conversation and I was lost, overwhelmed with grief so deep and filled with tears that flowed so hard they could fill the creek next to our family burial plot. The very creek where she taught me how to crab. The woman born Martha Ann Heyward, the granddaughter of Abraham Heyward—assigned Slave Cabin #11 on the Heyward Plantation in the 1860 United States Census—left this world without me and transitioned to the next.

A moment of joy filled the church that Tuesday morning as we celebrated her life. Her closest friends were her fellow choir mates who sang at their Baptist church every Sunday as well as at some weeknight Bible studies and revivals. These friends began to set up drums and a guitar, and someone pulled out a tambourine. They all wore beautiful electric royal blue dresses which they said was their color. I had known my grandma's favorite color to be purple. They revealed to the entire church—so packed there was standing room only with people spilling out into the parking lot—that they were in a rock band.

I smiled so big sitting there in that pew after sobbing for what felt like an eternity. Those women played and sang so beautifully. I longed for my grandma. I longed to tell her that I loved her and was proud of all of her, even the hellcat—especially the hellcat. All those years of me writing and directing music and attending band camp, and she didn't say anything about her own musical background. Nonetheless, I am her legacy.

My grandma was a Hellcat, and so am I.

I'd like to share a short fiction work that reimagines life on the Sea Islands in the 1960s for my grandma Martha and her good friends Lillian and Betty, in her all-girls rock band as told from the pages of her diary.

Rock on, Grandma, rock on!

December 31, 1961

Ridgeland, South Carolina

We sing at church tonight for Watch Night Service, but me, Lillian, and Betty are gonna go play in Cherry Hill! I've been helping my Aunt Lou with the fried chicken, collard greens, and Hoppin' John all day, so I haven't had much time to practice. Betty has taken a likin' to the guitar while Lillian has been playing the piano. I like the drums myself. They feel more magical, and I get to sit down after being on my feet in the kitchen all day! We all sing just fine. At least Lester says I have a nice singing voice.

January 1, 1962

Ridgeland, South Carolina

We sho' did have a swell time! Me and my girls, we brought the house down last night! Well, this morning! I thought I would've been too tired after listening to Deacon Henry shout WATCHMEN up until midnight. We were able to sneak off from Old House on over to Cherry Hill and put on our show. We sang one of my favorite songs from the Aretha record. She's the same age as us, I think. I wonder if we can make a record or go on the road someday.

February 10, 1962

Ridgeland, South Carolina

It's been a while since I wrote something down in here. I snuck off to see Lester on St. Helena Island by taking out Ma Josephine's bateau. We got a lot of folk we kin to over there but they just gettin' some bridges up. I don't think we need no bridges at all. It's fa buckra it seem like since we know the water. I've been goin' out on the ocean by myself since I finished grade school and probably with my granddaddy Abraham since I crack teet, ha!

March 2, 1962

Ridgeland, South Carolina

Today makes one year since we went to Columbia to protest at the State House. The year before we went to sit down at all those diners with "whites only" signs in da windows. Ma Josephine n Uncle Tinny told us not to go. So many people were jailed that day. We ain't get in too much trouble since we wore our nursing uniforms n was helping people who got hurt. Lillian led the songs most folks know. We shall overcome is my favorite.

May 16, 1962

Chicago, Illinois

I finally finished nursing school! I had ta come all the way up here to da Windy City, but dis is the top nurse training program in the country! Ma Josephine won't let me stay even though she moved up here for my learning. She's gonna stay since she met a man named Edward. Now her papa, my granddaddy Abraham, is sick. So, I'm gonna go back home to South Carolina to stay with him for a while to nurse him back to health. Funny thing is I'm just gonna make him some tea with some of the herbs in my garden when I get it growing again! Me n the girls got some shows to play up on the Chitlin' Circuit. If we win the local contest this summer then we might even make it to the Regal Theater. I wanna make it, n play my drums n sing, all the way to the Royal Theatre in Baltimore! We gonna have BIG fun in Baltimore!

May 25, 1962

Charleston, South Carolina

I made it back home just in time fa Decoration Day.
This year we honor de ooman souljahs who fought
during the Civil War. They was healers like me – Susie
King Taylor n Harriet Tubman. They used ta carry
'round herbs in they medicine bags ta heal soldiers. I
planted some of dem same herbs in my garden. I still
need practice makin' my med'sin. It's like root magic.
Music make me think of magic too. I don't think Ma
Josephine think so; she don't know I play drums. It's
still doing somethin' with my hands– just like sewing,
cooking, cleaning, n healing. It's somethin' about
drums that's healing. Feels like the beats awaken our
ancestors. I feel protection in the rhythms. It's
magical, rhythms n root work. I want Ma Josephine to
see me play. Maybe if I play at the Decoration Day
parade. Betty can bring her guitar, but I don't kno
how Lillian will play piano. Maybe we can surprise Ma
Josephine after the memorial church service. Lester n
my cousin Bo can help. Bo is sweet on this gal named
Ida. She a seamstress that come by the hospital. She
make our uniforms n fix the hems from time to time.
Bo say she can sing n she got some dance training at
that fancy dance theater in New York. Maybe she can
teach us some dances too! We done the twist one time
too many. Mr. James Brown, The Flames lead singer,
is from down here in the Lowcountry n he loves ta do
dem other popular dances like da camel walk, the
mashed potato, n da popcorn. We gone open for The
Flames one day.

June 8, 1962

Ridgeland, South Carolina

What I ain't have time ta grow after gettin' home from Chicago, I done had to forage. I feel it in my bones like I'm forgettin' somethin'. Granddaddy Abraham don't look too good. Ma Josephine is countin' on me. I don't wanna phone her since she got her hands full with my sisters. I can do this. I got everything I need... I gotta get some honey from Cherry Hill. Oh, n some cod liver oil too...

Mullein (Verbascum thapsus)
Peach Leaves (Prunus persica, Amygdalis persica (Linn.).
Persica vulgaris Null.)
Life Everlasting (Pseudognaphalium obtusifolium)
Elderberry (Sambucus canadensis)
Lavender (Lavandula angustifolia)
Rosemary (Salvia rosmarinus)
Peppermint (Mentha piperita)
Sage (Salvia officinalis)
Pot marigold (Calendula officinalis.)

June 14, 1962

St. Helena Island, South Carolina

I let Lillian n Betty convince me to take Ma Josephine's bateau. She fixin' ta be so worried when she see I'm gone. When Lillian set her mind on somethin' she keep it set! She want us to play at a festival over here. We stayin' with Lester in Land's End. It's nice n quiet. We got plenty of space to practice at branch church. They have a piano n a nice drum set. Betty brought her aunt's guitar. I hope we don't get into trouble. We bein hellcats.

You, Woman of a Certain Age

by Glenis Redmond
Pair with 2019 Brendel Noble One Chardonnay

You	red
You	orange
You	bloom
You	hum
You	doubt
You	fall
You	fail
You	frail
You	flail
You	fear
You	flinch
You	fester
You	crawl
You	climb
You	drive
You	driven
You	sly
You	slick
You	sick
You	really sick
You	cry
You	fight
You	double down
You	dream
You	fly
You	write
You	life

You	light
You	sing
You	dance
You	swing
You	sway
You	stomp
You	pray
You	chant
You	hear
You	hope
You	live
You	give
You	fire
You	ground
You	water
You	wind
You	Mama
You	Gaga
You	Poet
You	woman
You	giver
You	lover
You	hover
You	sky
You	try
You	survive
You	thrive
You	alive
You	resist
You	whirl
You	unfurl
You	breakthrough
You	beauty
You	inspired

You   inspire
You   flower
You   bloom anyhow!

The Day Our Lives Changed Forever

by Lizzie Outing
Pair with 2022 Regal Rose (Lovelee Wines)

It was 1992, and our lives were going pretty well for a normal family. My husband, George, and I were living the "American Dream." The children were gone and we could just up and go whenever we wanted to.

Then I got a call from my daughter, Jerilyn. She informed me that her sister, Sheila, had called her and said she found a lump in her breast and had gotten a mammogram. Sheila knew her mom well. She knew I would panic and go running to the doctor, and she wanted to handle this herself. She didn't want me to be upset. We went to the doctor together. He examined her and told us she needed a biopsy but not to worry about anything because she was too young to have cancer.

For the next week or so, we went on with our lives and did not worry about anything. Finally, the day came. She and I laughed and talked before she was wheeled into the operating room. Her doctor told me it would take about 40-45 minutes, so I proceeded to the waiting room. You know, there's something about the waiting room. You keep looking up to see if your doctor is coming as you watch other doctors come in and talk to people. You can tell when it's good news. The families laugh and shake the doctor's hand.

That morning, sitting there waiting and watching people coming and going, wondering why it was taking so long, I began to pace up and down the hall. After an hour or two, Sheila's doctor finally came out, but he wasn't happy. I could tell by his face that he had bad news. He asked to speak to me in another room, I don't remember much of what he said. All I heard was the word CANCER. I started to cry, and a nurse came in and sat with me. I wanted to pull myself together before I saw Sheila. I didn't want her to see my tears.

After some time, I felt as ready as I would ever be. I washed my face, put my glasses back on, and went to the recovery room. Sheila looked at me with her big, pretty eyes, waiting for answers. "Where were you when I woke up?" she asked. I lied and told her I had gone to get something to eat.

Her doctor had not come in yet with the news, so I sat next to her bed and said, "Sheila, sometimes things don't turn out like we expect. Whatever happens, we will work it out." She's a very strong young lady and accepted the news well.

Months later, we talked about that day, and she said, "Mom, I knew you didn't go get something to eat. You would never leave me!" She also told me that she knew something was wrong when I didn't come to see her right away.

Our church was on the way home from the hospital, so we decided to go in to pray. The door was locked, so we turned to leave. Just then, our minister, Rev. M. E. Dowell, rode up. He asked us to go back inside, and the three of us hugged, cried, and prayed together. From that moment on, we shared a special bond I will never forget.

Then reality hit. This was cancer and we couldn't send it back—we had to deal with it. And that's exactly what we did. Whenever Sheila had a doctor's appointment, I was always there, even if it meant leaving work. During her treatment, we sat and told jokes and made the best of those days with the other patients and their families.

We met like this each week with the same people. Some get better, graduate, and leave with balloons, while their loved ones laugh, cry, and hug them. You know you won't see them again, but you're so happy for them and can't wait until it's your turn to get those balloons. Then there are times you don't see someone for a while, and you know they're no longer with us.

After months of chemotherapy, Sheila finally got those beautiful balloons! She gave them to me, because she said I graduated with her.

Sheila went back to work and was doing well. We were so happy that things were back to normal, her cancer was gone, and we could resume our lives. She was dating a pharmacist who was very supportive and understanding. She loved to travel, and they took trips to the beach and mountains.

Christmas of 1992 was a happy time for our family, and we decided to have a big Christmas party with lots of food, drinks, dancing, and Christmas carols. We had no idea it would be our last happy Christmas. Sheila was always very quiet, the one who watches everyone else dance. Once she got cancer though, it's like she said to herself, "I'm going to enjoy life!" That night she danced so much that we all looked at each other amazed to see her having so much fun.

Sheila had a handful of friends with similar personalities, professional clothes, nice apartments, and sports cars. I laughed at them because they would go to a club every evening for happy hour, so they wouldn't have to cook. Sheila would eat, then come home and watch TV—that was her life.

Sheila met Mark in December 1992. He was different from other guys she had dated, and my husband, George, did not approve of her choice. George owns a barber shop and met Mark there. He had a reputation as a manipulator. But Sheila talked her dad into giving Mark a chance.

Sheila wanted a church wedding, and our minister counseled them beforehand. He asked Mark if he would stick by Sheila if she got sick again, and he said yes. They got married in February 1994, and Sheila was the prettiest bride you've ever seen. She got pregnant right away, and within a month, Mark was back to his old ways—staying out late, telling lies, sometimes not coming home at all and making up all kinds of excuses. Sheila knew what he was doing but kept it to herself.

And then her cancer came back.

In November 1994, she gave birth to baby Markus. Mark didn't help with the baby, he was never home, and he wouldn't pay the rent. He eventually moved away to be with another woman and Sheila finally gave up on him.

She has always been independent, so it didn't take long before she was back on her feet. She got a bigger, better apartment, new furniture, and a new car. She was back to her old self—except for the fact that she had cancer. Her illness didn't get her down though, and she was so strong. She never complained, always had a smile on her face, and you couldn't even tell she was sick.

That year she spent with her baby was the most wonderful year—her first Mother's Day, and Markus's first Thanksgiving, Christmas, and New Year. We recorded it all. Sheila kept so many things to herself. She asked me to get her a diary. I knew she wanted to keep a record of the things she could not talk to me about. She started making plans for Markus and telling me the things to do when he turned two—getting his booster shots and making a will.

I found myself spending more time with Markus as Sheila didn't want him to stay with her. Pam, my oldest daughter, took Markus to daycare, and I would pick him up to spend time with his mom. Sometimes we spent the night, and other times we went home. Sheila always had clothes packed for him.

One day at the cancer center, I told the social worker that I couldn't understand why Sheila didn't want to keep Markus at home with her. I knew how much she loved him. The social worker told me that Sheila was trying to bond Markus and me together. And that's exactly what she did.

Somehow Markus knew that the apartment was for playing, and my house was for sleeping. He loved his mommy and fell into our routine well. I loved taking him to see Sheila in the evenings. He would run into the apartment with his arms open and hug her around her neck. On nights she didn't feel well, he would go to her bed, wrap his arms around her and kiss her head. She always smiled for her baby, even when she was in pain.

In March of 1995, Anthony, a young man Sheila dated in high school, came back into her life. She confided in him and told him that she was sick. They were the best of friends. He would take her shopping, out to eat, and even clean her apartment. She was happy with him.

As spring approached, Sheila got sicker and her treatment got stronger. The doctor had little hope that she would get better, but she kept smiling and enjoying Markus, the apple of her eye. This was when I started wearing two faces—a smiling face when I was with Sheila and tears all the way home. There was nothing I could do to take away my child's pain. Even writing this, I have to stop to wipe away tears.

June came and Sheila was not getting any better. We went to my sister's one day and had so much fun. It was the last time we went out. I noticed that she was sleeping more and talking about my father who had died in 1982. That Sunday I made her favorite meal, but she wouldn't eat it. I asked her if she was feeling bad. She said no and to stop worrying about her and just take care of Markus. I called hospice.

The next day she was still saying she was okay, but we had a family meeting and decided we would stay with her 24/7. My sister Almetha would stop in, and Sheila was always happy to see her. George had stopped going into Sheila's room. He couldn't take it.

That evening Markus ran in and hugged her like always and she hugged him back. He had just learned to say, "I love you." She said, "I love you too,

Markus." Those were the last words Sheila ever spoke. The minister came that night and prayed with her.

On Wednesday morning, she was quiet and couldn't get up. I knew we were losing the battle. I told George he had to talk to his child before it was too late. It took everything he had for him to make those steps to her bed, but he did it.

Anthony came and sat by her bed and held her hand for hours. She began to grunt in pain. I sent Anthony to the store, and I got in bed with Sheila and held her in my arms and asked God to send his angels down and take my child home. She looked up in my face, closed her eyes, and went home.

I weep for my child because I miss her so. I weep for my child because of the short time she spent with her child. But I'm so grateful for the 28 years I got with her. I held her in my arms when she was born, and I held her in my arms when she died. Oh, what a beautiful death!

For a while I was in so much pain I stopped going to church. I didn't understand why God had taken my child from me. It took a message from my minister to remind me that I still had so much to be thankful for—my loving family and a beautiful little boy to take care of.

I want to say thank you to my minister and fellow church members, my co-worker Mary and my friend Carolyn, my kids—Pam, Jerilyn, Tim, and George III—and my wonderful husband. They were all there for Sheila as she bravely fought her battle.

I found this after Sheila's death:

Dear God,

I am going to leave this world. Give me strength, Lord, that I might not fear. I know, dear Lord, that if I do die, I shall continue to live in your arms, in your mind, in your spirit forever.

My heart breaks to be leaving those I love, my friends, my sisters and my brothers, my parents, and my little Markus. And yet, I know, I shall not be leaving. Heal my heart that I might know this. Heal theirs also that they might know we are bound together forever, through your power, which is greater than the power of death.

Let me feel the angel's tenderness as I exit this world and enter the next. Please comfort me and those I love. Let me see truth and know your peace. May my family and friends now feel the same.

Our love is larger than death, our bond is eternal. Bless my family, take care of them, my darling ones. Take me home, I shall not fear, you are with me. The cord that binds us one to the other cannot be cut, surely not by death. Jesus did not die when He did, and neither do we.

SHEILA

Praise How the Ordinary Turns Sacred

at Sam's on Woodruff Road
by Glenis Redmond
Pair with 2000 TOKAJI ASZÚ 6 PUTTONYOS

Praise to my drawing lines
I only buy paper towels in bulk,
so off to the Sam's (from now on it will be Costco) I
go,
when I got there my needs
turned into a bottle of wine and two dresses
for my about-to-be-born granddaughter
and a pair of stretch pants for my daughter after
delivery.
Praise to the cashier who carded me today.
I asked her if she did not see me standing here
with all this gray in my hair?
Praise to Black women.
Praise to her response: I see you and it.
I also know young folks
wear gray in their hair these days.
I said thank you for that compliment.
Praise to her smooth easy way
that did not miss a beat.
Grocery item. Check.
Compliment. Check.
Wisdom. Check.
Praise to her gray hair.
Praise to her age: 70.
I know her age because she told me.
She didn't look it.

65

She defied it
with the lightest of caramel hue.
Praise to her being comfortable in her own skin.
I just said, "I love us.
Love how we do."
She smiled and said thank you too.
Praise to slick elders.
Praise to when like meets like.
Praise to the pat on the back.
Praise to being seen and seeing.
Praise to it don't take much
And it don't cost you nothin.
Praise to some people have jobs,
other people on a mission.
Praise to the Vitamin D givers.
Praise to the admiration and the uplift.

Honoring My Truth

by Rian N. Jenkins
Pair with HER Essence (HERitage Wines)

Diamonds wish they could eclipse my radiance.
Rubies fall short in comparison to my worth God
created in heaven.
Before the world began . . .
    He envisioned the life
    Covered in purpose and blessings
    Molded in His magnificence.
    Wonderfully and beautifully handcrafted me
     into a reflection of greatness.

I won't allow perverted admiration
    to dilute or diminish my perception:
    I am a goddess
       queen
       warrior.
A woman of substance who is
     slaying demons more than fashion trends.
Intentionally uplifting this world with my brilliance.
Purposely, executing the plan.
Illuminating this Earth.
Eradicating the darkness.
Casting down every curse.
Breaking shackles.
Reviving the dead.
Invading prisons unlocking anyone who will listen.

The world is crying out.
I, we can't bow out.

Rest is needed.
Yet, we won't allow our grievances to silence us, bury
us.
Our voice is needed to boldly declare
    everyone can exude this glorious strength.
A power that won't let anyone devour our humanity.

Unity is the formula needed to forge a path of
resilience.
Don't have time to be stingy when God has freely
given us everything.
Blessed to be a blessing.
Abundance was never meant to be hoarded.
Ensuring no needy among us.
Prosperity is a river flowing, nourishing everything in
its path.

Heartache, tragedies may shake us.
Hope will reshape us, reminding us we are
overcomers.
Divinely equipped to handle any and every hardship.

Again, we are giants on the earth.
Tenacity is our stature
Securing the foundation
Building and sustaining nations.
Dismantling anything rooted in hatred.
Marching to a cadence that will prevail.

Conclusion

Pair with Tawny Port (Quevedo)

Black women being loved
and unapologetically joyous
taking up space

Mouths open wide,
releasing everything
through their laughter

Head thrown back,
eyes closed
You breathe when you laugh
until you can't

I truly believe in the power of storytelling. In my previous life, I used to work with survivors of sexual assault and relationship violence. As a survivor myself, and working with these courageous women, I witnessed firsthand the way storytelling had the power to bring people together and change the way we talk about something as devastating as sexual violence.

I left that work not because of the weight of the stories I was hearing day in and day out; I left because of the way the system wasn't there to truly serve survivors and how the system exploited my passion for this work. I felt like I could make more significant change in my community, on all levels, by doing my own community work through stories and storytelling.

I knew I wanted to be involved with this *Wine About It Anthology* project because so much of my work centers around bringing people, especially Black women, together through telling their stories. Through my work with my bookstore, Liberation is Lit, I partner with people in my community to use stories and storytelling as a way to build empathy, be vulnerable, and find connection in a world that wants to keep us so divided.

Curating the stories that are a part of this anthology was a joy. I felt connected to these women in ways I never thought I would. I admire their vulnerability in sharing their pain and showing how they came out on the other side. I wasn't expecting some of these stories shared here, yet they were all a beautiful tapestry of the experiences of Black women across the lifespan.

Black women are not a monolith; we do not all have the same experiences, yet we remain connected. Black women are not superhuman; we are vulnerable creatures determined to survive in a world intent on breaking us. We deserve love and care, from the world, but first and foremost from ourselves.

Thank you to all of the contributors who shared the stories close to their hearts. Thank you to Andrea for breathing life into this project. Thank you to the SC Arts Commission and the community for investing in the well-being of Black women across South Carolina. *Wine About It* isn't just a book; it's a movement to create a soft landing for Black women across our state.

Yours in Solidarity,

Tayler

Contributor Bios

Yaz Balogun

As a queer black woman living in South Carolina, it took me a long time to feel like I fit in with my family or the rest of the world. Ever since I found my community and started to express myself through art, every word feels like a victory call to my younger self. A lot of my poems are about healing from internalized misogynoir, fatphobia and homophobia. However, everything I write is inspired by love - romantic love, self-love, platonic love, unrequited love, et cetera. When you read my poetry, I hope you feel seen and I want my words to fill you with love and hope more than pain and despair.

Curtrell Gadson

Curtrell Gadson, is a healer, lover, joy seeker, relationship expert, and the community's auntie, who's a native of Columbia, South Carolina. She grew up oftentimes feeling invisible in her adolescence and relied on writing to cope. She's now rediscovering this lost art form of hers that she once enjoyed as a child and exploring all the many things she needs to say. Aside from writing, she enjoys cooking and hosting those nearest and dearest to her heart and spending time with her family and friends having the deepest laughs and fullest hearts.

Mikeya Janee'

Mikeya Janee' is a creative music artist, writer, speaker, and entrepreneur. She wholeheartedly pursues her passions with the belief that anything is possible. Her first self-produced projects include On Everything I Love and its sequel On Everything I Love: Affirming Me, a poetry and affirmations album. However, her music journey began earlier with the release of her debut album, 17-24, in June 2019. Four months later, Mikeya was cast as Michelle in the Dreamgirls musical at Florence Little Theater, and three years later, she released her EP Love's Orbit, which is available on all digital platforms. Outside of music, Mikeya is the owner of the Go Sis Movement holistic fitness community and the author of the Throne Talk Society Podcast. She also recently released a short story ebook entitled I'm No Superhuman: A Self-Love Short Story. You can learn more about Mikeya, her endeavors and establishments at www.mikeyajanee.com.

Rian N. Jenkins

Rian N. Jenkins is a phenomenal queen who believes in utilizing every gift God has bestowed on her. As a poet, she has evolved into a spoken word artist who has performed at numerous events and venues starting with events on Winthrop University's campus. Later, she adopted the nickname Anointed Misfit, which explains her motto: she is purposed by God to speak words that edify, motivate while tearing down myths that will prohibit anyone from living their best self. Over twenty years later, she was able to permanently ink empowerment in three self-published poetry anthologies. Those poetry anthologies are just the start of a long list of written published words she will produce.

Annait LJ

Annait is a 25-year-old military soldier who believes American Sign Language should be a standard practice. She centers her debut novel around an alternate earth where ASL is the primary form of communication. Annait grew up in Dekalb County, Georgia before moving to South Carolina with her family. She's been in and out of college working of her Bachelors Degree in Forensic Psychology. Between the gaps of her studies, she's worked full-time and part-time jobs, went on active duty orders to assist with the COVID pandemic response, and deployed overseas to Africa for a humanitarian relief mission. She intends to keep writing books and living life on her terms, taking it one day at a time.

Tracey Oakman

A former princess, daughter, sister, mother, grandmother, and friend, I've nurtured countless children with love and faith. My journey, rooted in the teachings of First Eternal Baptist Church, has led me to found Princess Empowerment and Boys to Men, dedicated to empowering youth. This lifelong passion reflects the legacy of my praying mother and loving father, who instilled in me unshakeable values. Through the ups and downs of life, my commitment to nurturing young minds has remained steadfast. I've poured into children the same love and guidance I received, ensuring a brighter future for generations to come. My work provides safe spaces for personal growth, combining mentorship, skill-building, and spiritual development to help young people reach their full potential. By fostering self-confidence, leadership, and critical thinking, we're shaping resilient, adaptable adults who will make a positive impact on the world. I am Tracey Oakman, from princess to queen.

Lizzie Outing

Liz Outing, 79, was born and raised in Columbia, South Carolina, during a time of profound change in the South. As a Black woman growing up in the segregated South, she witnessed and overcame immense challenges—yet her spirit remained unbroken. A devoted wife, loving mother of five, and retired teacher, Liz dedicated her life to nurturing both her family and the minds of countless students. Her compassion, strength, and unwavering love became the foundation for generations to come.

Whether in the classroom or at home, she led with quiet determination, teaching not just from textbooks but from the wisdom of lived experience. Her legacy is one of resilience, faith, and the enduring power of kindness—a testament to the countless mothers who turned struggle into strength. Today, her warmth, wisdom, and the lessons she imparted continue to shape the lives of those she held dear.

Glenis Redmond

Glenis Redmond is the First Poet Laureate of Greenville, South Carolina. She is a Cave Canem Alumni and Baldwin for the Arts Fellow. She is a Poet Laureate Fellow selected by the American Academy of Poets, 2023. Glenis has published six books of poetry. Her latest books are The Listening Skin(Four Way Books), Praise Songs for Dave the Potter, Art by Jonathan Green, Poetry by Glenis Redmond (University of Georgia Press), The Song of Everything: A Poet's Exploration of South Carolina's State Parks. Glenis received the highest arts award in South Carolina, the Governor's Award, and was inducted into the South Carolina Academy of Authors in 2022. The Listening Skin was shortlisted for the Open Pen America and Julie Suk awards.

Dr. Ebony Toussaint

Dr. Ebony Toussaint, PhD, MPH, MSN, RN is a Registered Nurse and Research Scientist who uses Afrofuturism and intersectionality in biosocial methods to advance health equity. She is Gullah Geechee and teaches the historical, social, and cultural impact of her culture in the American South. Dr. Toussaint's research incorporates her foodways and faith, including how Gullah Geechee people use plants to prevent illness and promote healing. When she's not working as an emergency nurse, she is consulting on and curating several comic books while co-hosting the Comic Book Community award-winning "Ororo Comics Podcast". She is the proud wife of Etienne Toussaint, Associate Professor of Law, and the blessed mother of their three children.

Wine Pairings

Introduction - 2018 Ericka O Syrah:
https://erikaobermeyerwines.co.za/product/erika-os
yrah2018/

Forewarned is to be Forearmed - 2020 Theopolis
Vineyard Petite Sirah:
https://www.theopolisvineyards.com/products/2020-
theopolis-vineyards-estate-grown-petite-sirah

Only Birthdays - B. Stuyvesant Heritage:
https://www.stuyvesantchampagne.com/product-pag
e/heritage-limited-edition

Raise a Glass - 2018 Bordini Barbaresco DOCG:
https://wilsondaniels.com/wine/bordini-barbaresco-
docg-2018/

I'm No Superhuman - 2021 "Solis" Malbec, Cahors
AOC, France:
https://thewineconcierge.co/products/2021-solis-ma
lbec-cahors-aoc-france

Falling in Love: The Gift that Keeps on Keeping On -
Aslina Chenin Blanc:
https://www.aslinawines.com/wines/chenin-blanc/

Beneath the Sentiments - 2021 Bayani Reserve - Pinot Noir (Stoney Wines):
https://www.vivino.com/US/en/stoney-wines-bayani-pinot-noir/w/7662042

The Miraculous Journey of a Princess: From Cellular Beginnings to Divine Purpose - 2023 Corazón Moon Mountain Gewürztraminer:
https://www.backroomwines.com/corazon-by-corison-gewurztraminer-moon-mountain-sonoma-2023

Hellcats - 2022 White Blend Daisy (FLYgirl Wines):
https://flygirlwineryllc.com/products/flygirl-wines-now-available/2022-white-blend-daisy-53187023

You, Woman of a Certain Age - 2019 Brendel Noble One Chardonnay:
https://www.wine.com/product/brendel-noble-one-chardonnay-2019/781045

The Day Our Lives Changed Forever - 2022 Regal Rose (Lovelee Wines):
https://thewineconcierge.co/products/lovelee-wines

Honoring My Truth- HER Essence (HERitage Wines):
https://www.heritagewinesllc.com/products/her-essence-red-wine

Praise How the Ordinary Turns Sacred - 2000
TOKAJI ASZÚ 6 PUTTONYOS:
https://leonandsonwine.com/products/2000-lenkey-pinceszet-tokaji-aszu-6-puttonyos-tokaj-hungary

Conclusion - Tawny Port (Quevedo):
https://quevedo.pt/en/product/tawny-port

About the Project

The Wine About It Anthology Series is a collection of stories focused on resilience, identity, and community, highlighting diverse voices and experiences from across South Carolina. Each volume showcases the diverse culture of the state with local narratives, celebrating storytelling, culture, and social justice. Paired with unique wine selections that enhance the reading experience, the series offers an immersive, sensory connection between literature and wine.

This collaborative initiative brings together Lit Between the Wines, Liberation is Lit, and Uncut Gems Agency to curate a dynamic experience that fosters community engagement, education, and empowerment. Each business plays a crucial role in uplifting underrepresented voices while promoting social justice through storytelling. The series culminates in Wine & Vinyl: A Multidisciplinary Art Exhibit, where literature, wine, and visual art offer a celebratory experience that reflects the rich cultural landscape of South Carolina.

Thank you to our generous donors and the South Carolina Arts Commission for funding this project.